SAY

WASTE

101 Easy Ways
to Create Less Waste

Harriet Dyer

summersdale

SAY NO TO WASTE

Text by Abi McMahon
Research by Annika Loh

An Hachette UK Company
www.hachette.co.uk

Summersdale Publishers Ltd
Part of Octopus Publishing Group Limited
Carmelite House
50 Victoria Embankment
LONDON
EC4Y 0DZ
UK

www.summersdale.com

Printed and bound in Malta

Printed on 100% recycled card and paper

ISBN: 978-1-78685-961-7

Substantial discounts on bulk quantities of Summersdale books are available to corporations, professional associations and other organizations. For details contact general enquiries: telephone: +44 (0) 1243 771107 or email: enquiries@summersdale.com.

Disclaimer
Neither the author nor the publisher can be held responsible for any loss or claim arising out of the use, or misuse, of the suggestions made herin.

CONTENTS

WHAT'S SO BAD ABOUT WASTE?

INTRODUCTION

Our earth is bursting at the seams with waste. Our landfills are, well, full – and swathes of beautiful earth and ocean are overflowing with stinking garbage. Heart-wrenching images of turtles' bodies warped by plastic, or birds' stomachs full of indigestible food wrappers and man-made detritus are unfortunately all too familiar today.

The good news is that there is something that everyone can do about it – and it's not that difficult to get started! This book will help you reduce waste in every area of your life, bit by bit. Here you'll find 101 little changes that can make a difference. And you can start to reduce the waste you personally produce and change the world one step at a time. Simply pick one of the tips and follow it for a week. If that works, continue for a month or add another idea, building on your success.

Successfully tackling our overproduction of waste comes down to the three main principles of recycling: reduce, reuse and recycle. This doesn't mean you have to sacrifice owning things! Instead, focus on ensuring that the products you buy have a small waste impact to start with and that they last a long time, being repaired or repurposed when they get worn out. This book will show you how to make better buying choices and guide you through the best techniques for brightening and bolstering your flagging items.

Finally, extra information has been added to each tip to help you decide if this waste-reduction method is best suited to your lifestyle. You'll see little icons on each page. This is what they mean:

KEY

This is cheaper than the wasteful alternative	This option is widely available on the high street	This is a do-it-yourself option	This option reduces the total waste you produce

This option is waste-free	This option extends the life of your things	Elements of this option are compostable	This option involves a new way to do things

A STAGGERING 2.12 BILLION METRIC TONNES OF WASTE IS DUMPED GLOBALLY EACH YEAR.

IN FACT, 99 PER CENT OF PURCHASES ARE BINNED BY THE SIX-MONTH MARK.

The UK throws away 7.2 million tonnes of food every year, more than half of which is perfectly edible. In the US an estimated 30–40 per cent of the food supply is wasted, with food waste accounting for the single largest waste source entering local landfills. Meanwhile, one in seven people across the world don't have enough to eat. Sadly, 1.3 billion tonnes of food is wasted globally each year. It is estimated that each consumer in the UK and the US wastes on average 100 kilograms of food a year.

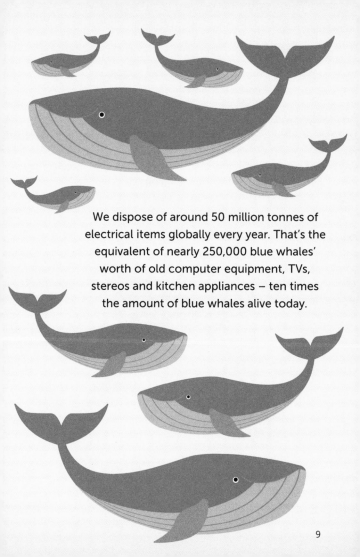

We dispose of around 50 million tonnes of electrical items globally every year. That's the equivalent of nearly 250,000 blue whales' worth of old computer equipment, TVs, stereos and kitchen appliances – ten times the amount of blue whales alive today.

Since its production first began in the early twentieth century, 8.3 billion tonnes of plastic has been produced, but only 9 per cent of that has ever been recycled.

UK music festivals alone generate around 23,500 tonnes of waste every year, of which only a third is recycled and the rest destined for landfills. Waste left behind includes drinks bottles, disposable cups and plates, food waste, leftover tents, sleeping bags and even non-biodegradable glitter.

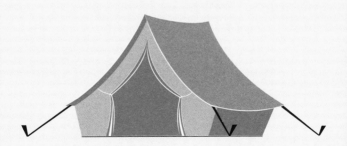

FAST FASHION TAKES A TOLL ON THE ENVIRONMENT. THANKS TO THE MULTIPLE STAGES OF MANUFACTURING AND TRANSPORTATION FOR JUST ONE GARMENT, THE CARBON FOOTPRINT OF TEXTILE AND CLOTHING PRODUCTION IS ENORMOUS. EVEN NATURAL FABRICS CAN BE PROBLEMATIC: IT TAKES OVER 5,000 GALLONS OF WATER TO PRODUCE ENOUGH COTTON TO CREATE A T-SHIRT AND A PAIR OF JEANS.

Christmas really is a time of excess. Every single year UK households alone throw away around 277,000 miles of Christmas wrapping paper while the US bins around 38,000 miles of ribbon.

BIODEGRADABILITY TIMELINE

5 days–1 month	**VEGETABLES**
2–5 months	**PAPER**
6 months	**COTTON T-SHIRT**
1–5 years	**WOOL SOCKS**
25–40 years	**LEATHER SHOES**
30–40 years	**NYLON FABRIC**
50–100 years	**TIN CANS**
80–100 years	**ALUMINIUM CANS**
500 years to forever	**STYROFOAM CUP**
500 years to forever	**PLASTIC BAGS**
1 million years	**GLASS BOTTLES**

BIOMASS IS PLANT AND ANIMAL WASTE
NOT CONSUMED BY HUMANS OR ANIMALS.
FORTY BILLION TONNES OF BIOMASS
IS PRODUCED GLOBALLY EACH YEAR.
THIS FIGURE IS EXPECTED TO RISE BY
50 PER CENT TO 80 BILLION TONNES
BY 2020, ROUGHLY THE EQUIVALENT
WEIGHT OF 174 GREAT PYRAMIDS.

THE WORLD'S POPULATION IS ON TRACK TO REACH 9.6 BILLION BY 2050. THE UN PREDICTS THAT IT WOULD TAKE THE EQUIVALENT OF THREE PLANETS' NATURAL RESOURCES TO SUSTAIN OUR CURRENT LIFESTYLES FOR A POPULATION OF THAT SIZE.

HEALTH AND BEAUTY

INTRODUCTION

Looking after your body can generate a lot of waste. Beauty, skincare and hygiene products are often packaged in non-recyclable containers and boxed in cardboard and plastic – not to mention the additional laminated sheets of instructions, applicators and even plastics in the products themselves. It can be tricky to be eco-friendly when you enjoy spending time and money on your appearance. Frankly, it can be hard to be eco-friendly even when you just do the bare minimum! Basic products like shampoo, toothpaste and deodorant need replacing often, and most of the products on the high street come in hard-to-recycle packaging. However, you'll be surprised by how much waste you can cut by scouting out cheap and easy-to-find replacements, or trying a little DIY magic.

1

NATURAL MAKE-UP BRUSHES

It is possible to be an eco-conscious make-up lover. Firstly, identify which aspects of your make-up produce the most waste. This is most likely to be the packaging for the make-up itself – the plastic pans and vials that are then packaged in cardboard boxes. Look for eco-friendly make-up brands that use recyclable materials such as bamboo or metal to package their products. Some brands also offer refills, which cuts out the production of unnecessary packaging and focuses on what's really important: the product inside. You can find make-up brushes made of recyclable materials such as bamboo or stainless steel in cosmetic stores on the high street.

2

SOAP BARS

Liquid hand soap and body washes packaged in plastic bottles – and sometimes sold in a cardboard box – inevitably generate a high quantity of waste. Avoid accumulating this bathroom waste by buying bars of solid soap. Select soaps that are packaged in non-waxed paper or recycled cardboard to divert your waste from the bin to the composter. There are plenty of suitable soaps available on the high street, ranging from fragrance-free bars for sensitive skin to designer soaps for those who like a bit of luxury. A bar of soap is not only eco-friendly but economical too; they last longer than most bottles of liquid soap – one pump often dispenses too much – so your stock won't need to be replenished as frequently.

DIY SOAP

Making soap at home is easy once you get started. Although it can mostly be made with items that you will already have in your kitchen, you will need to buy some equipment and ingredients, such as soap moulds, heat-resistant glass pitchers and lye flakes. You can find full lists of necessary equipment, plus free recipes, online. However, once you've made your initial purchases, soap making becomes the cheaper and eco-friendly alternative to buying ready-made soaps. You only need to replace the lye flakes and any perfumes or scents that you would like to include. Adding your own scents, colours and decorative elements, such as dried flower petals, is also part of the fun of soap making.

BAMBOO TOOTHBRUSHES

An easy win in reducing the waste you produce is to check the packaging of your standard toothbrush. Most toothbrush bristles are made of nylon and are not recyclable at all, but many big-brand handles are now made from recyclable plastic. If you would prefer to avoid the carbon footprint involved in plastic production altogether, try bamboo toothbrushes. Available online or in big-name supermarkets, bamboo toothbrushes are often packaging-free or use cardboard packaging, and are both recyclable and compostable. Most bristles on bamboo toothbrushes are nylon but some are fully compostable. Beware of the fully compostable variety if you want to avoid animal products, as the bristles are often made from pig hair.

5

MISWAK STICKS

Miswak sticks are herbal chewing sticks that have been used as part of oral hygiene routines in places such as the Arabian peninsula, North Africa and parts of Central and South East Asia. It's thought that they have been used by humans to clean their teeth for over 7,000 years. The miswak stick has antibacterial properties, which help reduce plaque and eliminate bad breath. You don't need to use toothpaste; simply chew the top inch of the stick until it has divided into bristles, soften the bristles in water and brush your teeth. When this section of bristles is used up, cut it away and start the process again. The sticks are compostable, so the waste won't contribute to landfill. They're readily available online at big-name retailers.

6

RID YOURSELF OF THE TOOTHPASTE TOOTHACHE

As brushing your teeth is a necessary part of your daily hygiene routine, toothpaste tubes and packaging can be a significant contributor to your impact on landfill. Most toothpaste tubes and dispensers are made of plastic and are non-recyclable, which is another reason to cross them off the shopping list. You can reduce this waste by swapping to solid, chewable toothpaste tabs. Simply pop a tab in your mouth, chew it up and start brushing with a wet toothbrush. The tabs are often packaged in compostable cardboard or recyclable plastic.

7

THE GREEN WAY TO WHITEN

You don't have to spend a fortune on whitening products and generate a one-person mountain of waste to maintain a pearly white smile. You might be surprised to learn that there are several common kitchen-cupboard items that are whitening aids. Brush your teeth with bicarbonate of soda once or twice a month to remove plaque and whiten your teeth. This method is so effective that some whitening toothpastes actually include bicarb in their ingredients. You can also utilize the ever-versatile coconut oil for whitening purposes. Swill a tablespoon of coconut oil around your mouth for 5 minutes and spit it out in the bin (the oil will clog the drains). Coconut oil has anti-fungal and antibacterial properties, which makes it a great organic mouthwash, and after two weeks of daily use you'll notice your teeth are comparably whiter.

8

DO THE FLOSS

Floss can be another little unnecessary addition to the general waste pile. Plastic floss packaged in a plastic box is a double whammy of future landfill. Even floss that looks like standard thread is actually made of nylon – it will take years and years to biodegrade. In the meantime, discarded floss litters the ocean, tangling up around sea creatures (such as seals) and cutting their skins. Swap plastic-based floss for silk floss that is packaged in glass or cardboard. Silk is very biodegradable and much kinder to the environment than nylon (although silk is not suitable for vegetarians or vegans due to the manufacturing method).

9

SOLID SHAMPOOS AND CONDITIONERS

Shampoo and conditioner are bathroom items that are used almost daily by most people. This means they get regularly used up and replaced, resulting in the manufacture of more and more plastic bottles, the majority of which are often not recycled. To combat this, try replacing your bottled haircare products with solid shampoo and conditioner. These blocks are often packaging-free or wrapped in compostable paper or card, and are easily available online or in high-street shops. There are plenty of solid shampoos and conditioners that target hair with particular requirements, such as dry, fine or oily hair, so you don't have to sacrifice looking good in order to save the planet.

10

COCONUT CONDITIONER

You can cut the cost of your haircare purchases by replacing the conditioning step in your regular hair wash with a twice-weekly coconut oil conditioning mask. Remember to buy your coconut oil in bulk; it will likely come in a plastic container, which is unfortunate, but as the oil can be used for so many different purposes you'll be able to eliminate dozens of other unnecessary bottles and packages from your waste. Warm a coin-sized flake of coconut oil in your hand and apply to your hair. Comb it through and, if your hair is long, loop it up into a loose bun at the nape of your neck. Leave on for 30 minutes and rinse thoroughly with hot water.

11

COCONUT EVERYTHING ELSE

A big jar of solid coconut oil really is a shortcut to waste reduction. Stay moisturized without racking up empty bottles of moisturizer by replacing them with coconut oil. As an alternative to make-up removal wipes, which are invariably non-biodegradable and end up in landfill or clogging drains, coconut oil is an eco-friendly choice. It should be applied directly to your face, removing the need for cotton pads and cotton wool. Simply warm a little in your hand, rub it on to your face and wash off with hot water.

12

SUN PROTECTION

Sunscreen is yet another addition to the many plastic bottles cluttering our bathroom cabinets – there are so many! Of course, sun damage is potentially very dangerous, so you shouldn't forgo wearing protection in the name of zero waste. However, you can alleviate the burden that it puts on the environment. Some of the chemicals found in sunscreen have been linked with the destruction of coral reefs, so opt for a product made from environmentally friendly ingredients (the active ingredient that will help protect you from sun damage is zinc oxide). Of these, several brands package their sunscreen in recyclable tins or compostable cardboard packaging.

13

SUN PROTECTION FOR CLOUDY DAYS

On days where the sun is out, but weak and partially obscured by clouds, opt to wear a hat to protect your head and thin, long layers to cover your arms and legs. This will shield you from the sun without having to use sunscreen, although you may choose to use a small amount to cover your face and exposed skin. The cover-up method has been used by humans who live in hot climates for thousands of years and is completely waste-free.

14

ALOE VERA FOR SUNBURN

Ouch! Sunburn really hurts! When you've caught the sun you need to do several things to avoid aggravating the burn and causing you more pain and discomfort. You need to cool the affected area, reduce the inflammation and moisturize the skin to combat that "tight" burn feeling. Aftersun lotion does all three, but is unfortunately packaged in plastic bottles. Replace your bottle of aftersun with a mature aloe vera plant. The next time you need burn relief, simply break off a leaf and spread the cool gel inside across the affected area. Surprisingly, refrigerated milk and yoghurt also help; the protein and the pH level help reduce inflammation, and the temperature obviously offers cool relief. Soak a flannel or piece of thin fabric in milk and apply to the burn.

15) SUGAR WAXING

This DIY hair removal technique has been used since 1900 BCE. Sugar is hypoallergenic and friendly to most skin types.

You will need: 170 g granulated sugar,
60 ml fresh lemon juice, 60 ml water,
handful 20 x 7 cm (8 x 3 in.) cotton strips.

Combine ingredients in saucepan over high heat, stirring continually with a wooden spoon. Constantly measure temperature and immediately take the pan off the heat when the mixture reaches 135°C/275°F.

Pour mixture into a sterilized glass container and leave to cool. Once cool, scoop out a spoonful and begin to knead it until it turns an opaque golden colour.

Apply to skin by pressing firmly onto the desired area until you have a thin layer of coverage.

Place a cotton strip over the wax and then pull quickly and firmly in opposite direction of hair growth.

Afterward, place strips into a bowl of hot water. This dissolves the wax and means that you can reuse the strips. You can store unused wax for the future.

16) BULK MASCARA

You can make your own mascara by mixing together ingredients that are packaged in glass bottles or that you have bought in bulk.

You will need: 1 tbsp activated charcoal, ½ tsp shea butter, 1 tsp bentonite clay, 2–3 drops oil, such as sweet almond or olive oil bought in glass bottles.

Mix all the ingredients together until fully combined and store in a sealed glass jar or bottle. You can save the wands from your empty mascaras and use them to apply your home-made product.

Sterilize old wands by soaking in warm (not boiling) water for 15 minutes to loosen the dried mascara and then isopropyl alcohol for 15 minutes to sanitize.

Scrub with soap and water, rinse and leave to air dry. Store in a dry cupboard.

17

BAMBOO DRY WIPES

Flushed wet wipes are one of the biggest contributors to the UK's clogged sewers. If you absolutely must use wet wipes to remove your make-up, make sure you dispose of them in your general waste bin. If possible, purchase bamboo dry wipes – they are biodegradable and can be disposed of in your composter.

18

MAKE-UP REMOVAL THE OLD-FASHIONED WAY

Even eco-friendly make-up removers such as bamboo dry wipes create some packaging waste that is destined for the landfill. Despite what the adverts say, you really don't need a lot of different products to effectively remove make-up. Simply scrubbing your face with a flannel or washcloth soaked in hot water will do the job. If you have sensitive skin that might react badly to being worked over with a rough fabric, try muslin. It's a lighter, softer material that will still successfully remove any traces of make-up.

19

ECO-FRIENDLY TAMPONS AND TOWELS

As if navigating your period wasn't challenging enough, there's the environmental impact to consider too. Neither plastic nor cardboard tampon applicators are recyclable, and some sanitary towels contain as much plastic as five plastic bags. With half the population in the world using these products, that's a lot of plastic waste. Fortunately, there are now more eco-friendly options readily available. An easy way to start cutting your sanitary plastic refuse is to use applicator-free tampons, of which there are many brands available in supermarkets. As most big-name sanitary brands have some element of plastic in their cotton mix, look online to find 100 per cent cotton tampons and pads.

20

SUSTAINABLE PERIOD SUPPLIES

There are sanitary products that eliminate single-use plastics and significantly reduce the waste you produce around your period. Firstly, you could try using cloth pads or absorbent underwear. There is a larger initial cost with these products, but simply pop them in the wash and they're ready to use again. If you are out and about and have a heavier flow then you might need to think ahead, as you can't dispose of the soiled pads or underwear. Secondly, you could try out one of the silicone cups that fit internally, such as the Mooncup or DivaCup. These can be worn for up to 8 hours, emptied, cleaned and used again, and last for up to ten years. Fitting and changing the cups may take a bit of getting used to, but this is a very eco-friendly method of managing your period.

21) DIY BODY LOTION

While the purchase of eco-friendly products can be helpful for the environment, it can also put a bit of a strain on your budget. When you're struggling to make the choice between the environment and your budget, try the alternative: the DIY option. This body lotion recipe uses items packaged in recyclable material or bought in bulk.

You will need: 2 tbsp grated beeswax, ½ cup sweet almond oil, 2 tbsp cocoa butter, 2 tbsp vitamin E oil, ¾ cup water.

Melt beeswax, almond oil and cocoa butter in a bain marie. Once they've melted, add vitamin E oil, which will act as a natural preservative and also nourish your skin.

Add the water to a blender. Set the blender to a medium speed and slowly pour in the oil mixture.

Once combined, add your mixture to a sterilized glass jar and store in a cool, dark and dry place for up to eight months.

22

DEODORANT

Deodorant is another necessary hygiene product that needs to be replaced often, resulting in a large volume of plastic waste over the course of the year. Although the high-street deodorant offerings are plastic-heavy, you can find eco-friendly deodorant options online. Green brands offer deodorant sticks packaged in cardboard or aluminium, which are recyclable materials, and some brands even offer refill services. Look in the more eco-conscious high-street stores for other waste-reduction options; some green brands offer bulk bottles of liquid deodorant that can be decanted into smaller spray bottles, or long-lasting deodorant crystals packaged in recyclable plastic. You'll still create some plastic waste when you purchase more deodorant, but one bottle should last much longer than the small roll-ons.

23

CLEAN HABITS

Water is a resource that we in the Western world take for granted. We consume a lot of clean water; the average Briton uses around 150 litres of water a day, through showering, bathing, cleaning, and so on. In the US the average daily water consumption per person is more than 300 litres. However, in parts of Denmark the average person only consumes around 80 litres per day, so a dramatic reduction of water consumption is possible. One method is to replace your shower head. Quick-flow heads and "power showers" pump through water at a faster rate, causing you to use more water over the same shower duration. Another method is to time your shower. An 8-minute power shower uses 137 litres of water. In comparison, a 5-minute shower using a low-flow shower head uses only 56 litres – a large improvement.

24

WATER CONSERVATION

You can take water conservation a step further and reuse your shower and bathwater for the garden. Maintaining a garden or plant pots can use a surprisingly large amount of water – around 7 per cent of the average person's water consumption (spread across the year) is through watering plants. Save water by showering with a bucket on the floor or by not draining your bath after you are done. Use the reserved water on your garden and plants. Experts say that this used water, known as "grey water", is healthy for your garden when augmented with clean water: soil and compost will filter out the detergents from your shampoo, conditioner and body wash. However, don't use grey water on edible crops as pathogens in the water may be absorbed by the plants and then consumed by humans.

25

SWAP PLASTIC SPONGES FOR BAMBOO BRUSHES

Synthetic sponges, nylon shower puffs and plastic loofahs all head directly to the landfill when discarded. The good news is that all three can be replaced with natural, biodegradable alternatives. Natural loofahs are made from dried luffa gourds and can be disposed of on the compost. Washing sponges were originally made from sea sponges; the technique for farming them is sustainable, but they are classed as animals – although they do not have a brain or central nervous system – so for some this is not a vegan or vegetarian choice. Many high-street stores sell bamboo brushes, the handles of which are compostable, and pumice stones can be used for life (you will need to clean them).

26

BUYING CLOTHING

As you can see on p.12, fashion is an industry that produces a lot of waste. Help to reduce your contribution to this industry by following this hierarchy of purchasing:

1. Buy second-hand.
2. If you can't buy second-hand, buy clothes made from recycled material.
3. If you can't buy recycled clothes, buy organic and fair trade clothes.

Avoid buying clothes made from plastic-based materials such as nylon and synthetic polyesters. These do not easily biodegrade, and simply clog up landfill.

27

FRIENDLY CLOTH

There are lots of eco-friendly companies that offer sustainable clothing, whether they use recycled cloth or sustainable materials. The term for this is "sustainable fashion" – searching for this online will bring up a lot of results and you're likely to find clothes that you like. Sustainable materials are those that use fewer resources during their farming and creation and will biodegrade at a quicker rate than plastic-based fabrics. These materials include hemp and bamboo, which are fast-growing materials that require less water than cotton (another sustainable material) to yield the same quantity. Rayon is a sustainable fabric that can be made to imitate other fabrics, including wool or silk, and is often mistaken for a synthetic fabric. It is in fact sustainably made from tree cellulose, making it eco-friendly.

28

HANG ON TO YOUR CLOTHES

One way to reduce your fashion waste is to simply wear your clothes for a little longer. For example, instead of throwing out clothes that are no longer in fashion, pair them in different combinations to make them work. Another way is to learn how to perform simple fixes on your clothes, so a lost button or a torn zip doesn't spell the end for a favourite shirt or pair of jeans. If you have the time and the aptitude you could even learn some basic tailoring skills, so you can re-cut and adjust clothes that have fallen out of fashion or perhaps shrunk in the wash. Don't forget that what's out of fashion now will probably be back in fashion in a few years – another reason to hang on to your clothes!

29

DISPOSE OF YOUR CLOTHES THOUGHTFULLY

If you are ridding yourself of unnecessary or unwanted clothing, dispose of it in an eco-friendly manner. Clothes that are in good condition could be resold or donated to charities, clothing drives or second-hand stores. If you have specialist gear and clothes relating to a hobby – anything from climbing to fishing, motor racing to athletics – and if high-street stores might struggle to sell it, search online for charities and not-for-profit organisations that would welcome donations. You will benefit not only the environment but also like-minded people, including young people and adults in developing countries, who might want to start a hobby but are not able to afford the start-up costs.

30

BUY SHOES RESPONSIBLY

Shoes really do take a beating; not only do they have to support our weight all day, but they also need to protect our feet from all the elements. The same rules for responsible sourcing and disposal apply to shoes as they do to clothes (see pp.45 and 47). You may also benefit from thinking carefully about how you shop for shoes. Use the money that you would spend on several pairs of flimsy fashion shoes on one pair of sturdy, practical shoes. Have the shoes' material treated to be water-resistant and regularly clean them so stains don't set into the material.

31

GROW AN APOTHECARY'S GARDEN

Many of the DIY suggestions in this book such as the soap bars on p.21 and the body lotion on p.39 can be scented and decorated with flowers. Instead of purchasing flowers wrapped in flimsy unrecyclable plastic, grow your own and dip into your flower patch whenever you need it. Lavender and roses are easy to grow and beautifully scented. Grow poppies and add their seeds to your soap bars as an exfoliator. When your aloe vera grows an offshoot, break it off and plant in a new pot so you always have a plentiful supply to add to your lotions. You can even expand your garden to nourish you in other ways: ginger is an easy-to-grow plant that can alleviate some nausea as well as pain during the menstrual cycle.

32

INVEST IN SOAP BERRIES OR "INDIAN WASH NUTS"

Soap berries, or "Indian wash nuts", have been used for thousands of years as a natural washing detergent by people native to both Asia and the Americas. They grow on trees of the *Sapindus* genus and are a source of saponin, a natural surfactant, which cleans and freshens your clothes. Soap nuts are gentle on your clothes – colours stay brighter for longer – while effectively removing dirt. Available online and in some alternative stores, these eco-friendly scrubbers are often packaged in cloth bags, ensuring your laundry routine makes even less of an impact on the environment.

FOOD AND HOUSEHOLD

INTRODUCTION

Do you often wonder why on earth fruit and vegetables need to be packaged in plastic, especially in supermarkets, when most of it is available loose? And when you do select loose items, why there are only plastic bags, and not paper bags, available for you to place them in? Thankfully, some supermarkets have started to acknowledge their impact on the environment and are starting to cut their packaging. This chapter will help you pick out the best shops to use and introduce you to ethical stores that are ahead of the curve and have eschewed packaging altogether. You'll also learn tips to help you cut waste once you've brought the food home, including the best methods for disposing of food waste, and top recipes to help you keep that waste to an absolute minimum.

EAT SEASONALLY

A lot of food waste is invisible to the average consumer; it takes place while the food is being harvested, packed up, transported and delivered. In some cases, between 20 and 40 per cent of crops is lost to damage while being transported. Food industries attempt to reduce this damage by piling on the packaging: shrink-wrapping individual fruits and vegetables, adding packing foam around boxes full of goods, and keeping certain foods frozen or chilled. The further the food has to travel and the longer it has to stay fresh, the larger the amount of packaging. Opt to eat seasonally and locally wherever possible. You'll eat more genuinely fresh foods that create a smaller carbon footprint and less landfill waste on the journey to your table.

34

TAKE YOUR OWN BAGS AND CONTAINERS

Some countries, including the UK, have banned shops from offering free plastic bags to customers. Even if free bags are still available in your country, opt to bring along cloth tote bags, backpacks or sturdy multi-use plastic bags to carry your shopping home. Maintain a stock of paper bags to bag up loose fruit and vegetables. Keep them in your car or your shopping bag so you have them on hand when you pop to the shops. You can even take along (clean!) plastic containers to put your deli-bought meats, fish and cheeses in. It might garner a strange look the first few times you ask, but supermarkets are becoming increasingly aware that being green is a big incentive for their customers and they are unlikely to refuse.

35

BUY LOOSE FRUIT AND VEGETABLES

If you are responsible for grocery shopping then you've probably noticed the rise in seemingly unnecessary packaging for fruit and vegetables. Some packaging apparently helps the consumer, such as shrink-wrap on cucumbers, which allows the vegetable to stay fresher for longer. Other packaging, such as plastic netting for onions or garlic, or bags for portions of ginger, helps the supermarkets by creating pre-weighed or sorted products for which they can charge more. If you compare the price of loose fruit and veg per kilo to packaged fruit and veg per kilo, you'll often find the loose option considerably cheaper. Cut the packaging and the price of your weekly shop by opting for loose fruit and vegetables every time!

36

EAT UGLY VEGETABLES

Supermarket standards focus far too much on the appearance of a fruit or vegetable; some farmers have up to 10 tonnes of produce a week rejected by shops, simply for not being attractive enough. Some of this rejected produce inevitably ends up in the landfill. You can help to change supermarkets' opinion of this "ugly" produce by buying misshapen and slightly bruised food, thereby clearing out the supermarkets' "odd" bin, and signing petitions that call for more ugly food. Some companies offer veg boxes that consist of the ugly fruits and vegetables rejected by supermarkets, and ironically some supermarkets offer the service themselves!

37

SHOPPING CHECKLIST

All this information about what to buy and how to buy it can be a lot to take in, so take a snap of the list below on your phone and consider these questions when you go shopping:

1. Do I have my bags and refillable containers with me?

2. Do I need to drive? If so, can I go with a friend?

3. Is it seasonal?

4. Is it locally sourced?

5. Can I buy it loose?

6. Is it packed in recyclable material, or is it in plastic?

7. Do I really need it? Is there an alternative?

38

GROW YOUR OWN

Growing your own food is the best way to eliminate food-based packaging waste. If you have a garden you can convert a sunny corner into a vegetable patch, or use containers to grow produce vertically and in tight spots. If you don't have a garden you can make use of both interior and exterior windowsills to grow food. If you have no outdoor space at all you can look into hydroponic growing – an indoor soil-free growing method. Home-grown fruit and veg might not completely replace the fruit and veg you normally buy from the shops, but you should be able to replace a portion of your weekly shop with home-grown produce. Needless to say, it's very satisfying to eat the food you've grown yourself.

39

WHAT DO I PLANT IN MY GARDEN?

Crops that grow well in containers include beetroot, broad beans, carrots, chillies, green beans, herbs, peas, peppers, potatoes, radishes, rocket, runner beans, salad leaves and spring onions. You can double your savings on landfill by upcycling old household items to serve as plant containers – tin cans, buckets and even old sinks can be transformed into homes for all sorts of crops. Peat-free compost is the eco-friendly choice for gardeners: peat is harvested from peat bogs, which are unable to naturally regenerate after the peat is stripped from them. Keep and crush eggshells to scatter over your garden to act as an all-natural, waste-free slug and snail repellent.

40

LEFTOVERS

Cooked food is not usually suitable for your home compost, so a waste-free household should deal with leftovers the old-fashioned way – eat them! One of the easiest and most cost-effective things to do with your dinner leftovers is to pack them up and have them for lunch the next day. Wet leftovers can go in bamboo containers or multi-use plastic lunch boxes, while dry leftovers can be wrapped in beeswax wraps or paper bags. Large quantities of leftovers can be chilled and then frozen to be eaten as a quick and easy meal at a later date. You can freeze more types of food than you might expect, including meat, fish, eggs, milk, cheese, bread, and fruit and veg (although these might go squishy when defrosted, they will still be good to eat). Check online to see how long food can be frozen for.

41

COOKING WITH SCRAPS

Although uncooked scraps of food such as fruit and vegetable peel can be composted at home, it's better to use as much of the food as you can before you start to dispose of it. Put your fruit scraps into water to create flavoured water. There are specially designed water bottles that contain a little "cage" for the fruit so you can flavour your water without the risk of swallowing an errant strawberry head! Vegetable scraps can be used to make a soup. If you're making a vegetable-heavy dish for dinner then it makes waste sense to cook a soup with the leftovers at the same time. You'll cook double the dishes in the same amount of time and you'll have a fresh meal ready for the next day.

42

FREEZE YOUR SCRAPS

The quantity of cooking waste will vary from meal to meal. You won't always produce enough scraps to transform into a soup from one session. Store these odds and ends in a bag or tub in the freezer and you'll soon have enough veggies to make your own vegetable stock. Onions, garlic and carrots are the perfect base for stocks and broths. You can even freeze onion and garlic skin, the green ends of spring onions and carrot peel for later use. Vegetables such as potatoes, peppers, mushrooms, celery and herbs such as sage, chives, bay or rosemary are also great additions to your stock scraps store. Avoid certain members of the brassica family, such as cauliflower, broccoli and Brussel sprouts, as these can add a bitter flavour to the mix.

43

BEESWAX WRAPS

Cling film is one of those products that appear to make life much easier but we can actually easily do without. It's a single-use plastic that is found in most homes, and a steady stream of it makes its way to landfill every year. Try using beeswax wraps to replace cling film for covering and sealing food in the fridge or transporting food in your bag. Beeswax wraps are reusable (after being rinsed in cold water), compostable and many come in attractive colours and patterns. They're as convenient as cling film too – simply warm the wrap with your hands to help it stick to a bowl or plate of food that you want to protect.

44

SEED SAVING

Starting your own kitchen garden doesn't have to equal massive start-up costs. In fact, you can source seeds from the very fruit and veg that you eat. Simply deseed the vegetables on your chopping board – courgettes, pumpkins, peppers and avocados are particularly good for this. Gardening books and websites will teach you how best to rear plants from seed. You can also plant old store cupboard veg that has sprouted, such as onions, potatoes and sweet potatoes. You can grow hardy onions all year round, so this is a crop that keeps on giving.

45

YOUR DAILY BREAD

Your daily or weekly bread purchase is a great opportunity to save on waste. Try buying from your local bakery. The bread should be packaged in recyclable paper rather than the plastic bag that most shop-bought bread comes in. If your local bakery doesn't use recyclable packaging, bring your own paper or cloth bag. An even more waste-conscious way to get your bread fix is to make your own. Varieties such as soda bread or focaccia don't need much, if any, proving and are quick to make. Buy your ingredients packaged in paper or glass and you'll be able to eat bread in the most eco-friendly manner. If you are time-poor but money-comfortable, a bread maker is a great investment. These machines do the mixing, proving and baking for you – simply pour in the ingredients and press go!

EVERY CRUMB HELPS!

Say goodbye to throwing away your old and stale bread ends. Recipes such as panzanella salad or bread pudding particularly require stale bread – and are great party foods! Even if you're only feeding your humble self, you can use up hardening bread by making some simple buttery toast (or a cheese toastie!). Stale bread can also be turned into croutons and stored in the freezer to later jazz up a meal. You can even grate or blend stale bread to create breadcrumbs (which are always overpriced in shops and yet you never have any to hand when you need them). Store the crumbs in an airtight glass container and use to coat mushrooms, meat or fish, or sprinkle them over gratins for a crispy topping.

47

PICK YOUR OWN

"Pick your own" farms allow you to pick fresh fruit and vegetables straight from the tree, bush or ground. Although they provide bags and boxes to carry the produce in, you can bring your own paper bags and sturdy containers. "Pick your own" farms are often the budget option for buying expensive fruits and vegetables – price comparisons are usually displayed on site so you can check you're getting a good deal. By picking the produce and transporting it home yourself, you'll cut out the invisible waste that comes with supermarket groceries. If you know your stuff you can even pick fruit from public land – but make sure it's public (to avoid the risk of trespassing on private land) before you start loading up with apples and berries. Blackberry brambles grow wild even in city areas, and blackberries can be frozen for future use.

48

THE JAMMY SOLUTION

Fruit that is starting to go off can be quickly cooked up into a fruit compote for dessert or a sweet treat. Compote is good on its own but can be served with a dollop of cream, ice cream or yoghurt. Soft and browning fruit will also make a good crumble or cobbler. If you don't want to create a dish to be eaten immediately, stew the fruit with sugar and some optional flavourings to create a jam or jelly. Pour into a sterilized jar and seal and you'll have something tasty in the cupboard for a rainy day. Soft fruits aren't the only ingredients you can use – add sugar and flavourings such as vanilla, ginger or lemon to sweet potatoes or butternut squash for a jam that sounds unusual but tastes delicious.

49

ZERO-WASTE MILK

Milk deliveries to your doorstep may have gone out of fashion but they're making a comeback, driven in part by eco-friendly and waste-conscious households. Although some deliveries include milk packaged in plastic, you can often opt for glass bottles which can be recycled – some services even take the bottles back to be used again. You can adjust how many deliveries a week you receive so you only purchase exactly the amount of milk required. If you find that you are regularly not using up your milk then you can turn it into yoghurt using a slow cooker. The process usually takes about 24 hours and is very low effort – you only need to spend some of that time checking on the cooker or transferring the yoghurt.

50

EVEN THE BONES

Not all leftovers can be boxed up and eaten for lunch the next day – you'd get some strange looks if you started gnawing chicken bones at your desk. However, they can still be saved from the landfill. Animal bones, such as chicken, lamb and beef can be cleaned, roasted and then boiled with water, herbs, vegetables and meaty offcuts to create a long-lasting broth or stock. Store the stock in the fridge and use it as a base for soups, casseroles, stews and other rich dishes. Vegetarians can make stock with similar leftover ingredients, minus the meat!

51

HOME-MADE SNACKS AND NIBBLES

Using leftover vegetables to make home-made nibbles saves on waste twice over: the veggies don't end up in your composter and the packaging from snacks doesn't fill the recycling bin or your general waste bin. Veggies such as carrots, beetroot, kale, green beans and parsnips can all be used to make tasty snacks using your oven or (a smart investment) a food dehydrator. There are plenty of recipes available online or in recipe books for both sweet and savoury nibbles. Store your home-made crisps in an airtight container in the cupboard.

52

BINS, BINS, BINS, BINS

Your kitchen should contain four different bins. This sounds like a lot but if you're worried about space, don't be – they don't have to be big bins. You should have one for waste glass, one for general recycling including tins and cans, one for compostable items and finally one for general landfill waste. Remember to check with your local authority for guidance on how to dispose of each kind of waste. As you incorporate more waste-cutting methods into your daily life you'll notice that your general waste bin will be much less full than your other bins – just what you want! Don't forget that you can put items such as unwaxed and uncoated paper and tissue into your compost bin. These will break down in your composter over time.

53

USE A WATER BUTT

A water butt is a receptacle that collects and stores rainwater, which can then be used to water your garden and indoor plants. Rainwater is better than tap water for most indoor plants as it has not been subjected to the same cleaning chemicals as tap water (to make it safe for humans to drink – plants have different tolerances to certain chemicals). The more water butts you have, the better, especially in hot summers where hosepipe bans may inhibit your ability to keep your veg patch healthy. The engineering-minded of you may be able to rig a system that siphons the water from your drains into your water butt. If you live in a rental property, do not attempt this as you may damage the building.

54

GO MEAT-FREE

Rearing, keeping, slaughtering and transporting farm animals for human consumption uses up a lot of resources compared to farming plant-based foods – it takes over ten times more fossil fuel to produce animal protein than plant protein. Animal agriculture also guzzles far more water; it takes anything between 1.5 and 6 times more water to produce a gram of meat protein than it does a gram of protein from pulses. Reducing or cutting your meat consumption can dramatically reduce your contribution to "invisible" waste and your carbon footprint. Seek out some of the many books or online resources about vegetarian or vegan lifestyles that can ensure you still consume all the nutrients you need, helping you go meat-free in a safe and healthy manner.

55

COFFEE BEANS AND LOOSE-LEAF TEA

Yes, there are even waste savings to be made when getting your caffeine fix. Coffee pods are famously non-recyclable, with every cup of coffee creating another addition to landfill (every two cups of coffee if you have the right machine). Eschew the pod and buy coffee in bulk. Laminated or foiled coffee packaging can't be recycled so buy coffee packaged in printed paper. Some specialist coffee shops offer coffee bean refills in paper or cloth bags. Check your favourite brand of tea to see if they provide compostable bags, as some teabags unfortunately contain plastic. Choose loose-leaf tea packaged in cardboard or paper where possible; this will cut out teabag waste altogether.

56

BETTER BUTTER

Swap butter packaged in plastic tubs for blocks of butter wrapped in paper. If you buy butter in plastic tubs because you prefer spreadable butter, simply store block butter outside the fridge for the same effect. Butter will keep as well in a cool, dry cupboard, especially when kept in a ceramic butter protector, and it spreads easily at room temperature. Some recipes require chilled butter but you can cut the required amount from the block and keep it in the fridge ahead of baking. Use any scrapings of butter left on the wrapper to grease cake tins when baking. The scrapings can even be used to apply fat to pans when frying ingredients such as eggs or garlic.

57

ALTERNATIVE SCRUBBERS

It's not just the packaging for cleaning products that gets regularly thrown away. While most kitchen cleaning implements aren't single-use plastics, they are often disposed of within three months. If you're looking to reduce plastic waste, buying a bristle brush or a sponge brush with replaceable heads can be a simple first step. Or, even better, you could revitalize your scrubbers. Clean and deodorize your kitchen cloths by boiling them or even zapping them in the microwave. You'll kill any bacteria and delay the need to buy another wastefully packaged pack. There are also plenty of products available online, such as bamboo bristle brushes. As with bamboo toothbrushes, the bristles themselves are plastic and non-recyclable, but the handles and heads are compostable.

LIFESTYLE

INTRODUCTION

A takeaway coffee here, a chocolate bar there – unwanted packaging can inadvertently mount up when you're out and about. Worse still, you are often out of reach of eco-friendly waste-disposal techniques, meaning that materials you would usually recycle become fodder for a one-material-fits-all bin... unless you want to carry your waste around with you all day! However, with a little forethought and preparation, you'll find that being kind to the environment when you're on the go isn't as hard as you think. This chapter contains lots of tips that will help you pack your bags with everything you need to keep going – plus a few treats. After all, you and Mother Earth are worth it!

58

WATER BOTTLES

Purchase a metal water bottle to carry with you on long journeys. It's estimated that a million plastic bottles are bought globally every minute, so you can knock a few bottles off that number by carrying your own bottle. Stainless steel bottles are preferable to plastic bottles as they are recyclable. The best option is to buy a bottle made from recycled stainless steel. Remember to wash your bottle between trips to keep it fresh and germ-free. The initial cost of a metal water bottle is higher than that of filled plastic bottles of water, but you'll soon make that back in savings.

59

PORTABLE COFFEE CUPS

Takeaway cups for tea and coffee rack up a lot of waste; while they may be made of paper and will biodegrade, often the paper is plastic coated and their plastic lids and stirrers will linger in landfill. Carry your own bamboo or steel travel mug with you and ask for your takeaway beverage to be served in that. You can purchase many different designs so they will not only make a waste saving but look more stylish than a takeaway cup. If you do enjoy carrying a branded takeaway cup, many big-name coffee shops offer their own to be purchased in store or online. An insulated flask works really well on car journeys, especially when topping up at coffee kiosks at fuel stations.

60

PACKED LUNCHES

It's time to go old school with your packed lunch! Eating pre-prepared lunches and leftovers will help you cut down on heavily packaged shop-bought sandwiches and ready meals. And packed lunches have never been cooler given the wide choice of beautifully designed bamboo and recycled stainless steel lunch boxes. You don't have to restrict yourself to a hearty sandwich either (although feel free to pack a sandwich if you love them); many designs include special compartments or sealed areas that allow you to safely pack leftovers or additional fruit slices or desserts. You could even pack delicious layered salads in glass jars – a tasty and aesthetically pleasing approach to going green.

61

CARRY METAL OR PAPER STRAWS

As more businesses are becoming aware of the negative impact of plastic straws, some are now offering paper straws as a fully compostable alternative. If you love drinking through a straw, or need one, then this is an eco-friendly alternative to plastic straws. You can even go one step further and carry with you a metal straw, or a handful of paper straws, when you're out and about. Simply remember to wash your metal straw at the end of the day, like you would your lunch box, and you'll always have a straw on hand. Think of it as a straw for life!

62

CARRY REUSABLE UTENSILS

Reducing your waste doesn't mean saying no to lots of fun activities. It means finding a way to take part in those activities while staying true to your green mission. If you fancy a tasty takeaway from a street vendor or food festival, simply carry your own metal utensils to avoid having to use the inevitable plastic disposable cutlery, which would linger in landfill for centuries. Wrap your utensils in a cotton handkerchief, beeswax wrap or cloth bag to prevent them getting dirty before you have your meal and to protect your bag or pocket from being dirtied after you've had your meal.

63

HANDKERCHIEFS

That's right – it's time to bring back cotton handkerchiefs. Paper tissues may compost in landfill but the plastic wrap they are packaged in won't – and cardboard boxes of tissues aren't terribly portable. If you carry a handkerchief with you, that's one less addition to the landfill or your composter. You can use this to blow your nose or wipe your hands if they get dirty. You can wrap your travel utensils in it – although you may wish to carry a separate hankie for this! You could also use handkerchiefs to dry your hands after using a public restroom, instead of the hand dryer or paper towels – again be careful not to muddle up your cloths!

64

CARPOOL OR USE PUBLIC TRANSPORT

You've heard that cars are bad for the environment because of greenhouse gases. You've heard that cars are bad for your health, and you should walk more. Well, now we're here to tell you that cars are bad for the environment, and particularly the oceans, because the slow wearing down of tyres produces microplastics that litter our seas. This is a global issue and one that is fairly new to the eco-agenda but, based on recent research, it deserves a higher place and priority on the political agenda than it currently receives. Carpooling, opting for public transport or walking or biking where you can will help slow the wear of tyres and ease the burden on the oceans.

65

BAKE YOUR OWN TREATS

Tray bakes such as flapjacks or blondies are quick to make and easy to portion out as your treats for the week. If you usually get peckish at work or simply can't survive the food shop without treating yourself, make sure you always have one of these treats at hand. They can be wrapped in beeswax cloth or packaged in a small bamboo tub and carried with you wherever you go. Health-conscious eco-warriors can slice up a small fruit salad as a treat for the same result.

66

CAFES, BAKERIES AND MARKETS

Break the bad habit of buying your treats-on-the-go from supermarkets and convenience stores. Their goodies are often packaged in plastics and foils to keep them fresh on the shelf for longer. Small cafes and bakeries display their wares under glass protection and make enough to sell that day only, so they do not have the same packaging problem. Ask these sellers not to package your selection. If you already have a box or wrap with you then you can put it in that. Look up farmers' markets in your area. You may be surprised what's taking place near you on any day of the week, but especially weekends. If you're out and about on a day you know a market is on, swing by and pick up a quick snack that's also packaging-free.

67

ALWAYS CARRY BAGS

You never know when you're going to need a spare bag – your existing bag might tear, you might make an impulse purchase, or a friend or colleague might surprise you with a gift. Carry a little foldable cloth bag on you at all times so that you never need to pick up a plastic bag when in a pinch. Many brands offer bags that fold down and clip together, so even if you don't carry larger bags, you can easily slip them into your coat or trouser pocket. Keep an eye out for "borrow a bag" initiatives running in your local stores. Groups such as Boomerang Bags offer reusable cloth bags that can be borrowed and returned when a customer has forgotten their own bag.

68

PREPARATION CHECKLIST

There is a lot to remember, so just like the shopping checklist (p.57) here is a checklist for you to run through when you're getting ready to go out. Being waste-conscious might mean you have to spend a little extra time getting ready, but it's worth it.

1. Have I filled and packed my water bottle?

2. Will I be eating out? Have I wrapped and packed my cutlery?

3. Will I be taking lunch? Have I packed my lunch box?

4. Have I packed my handkerchief?

5. Have I packed my spare bag(s)?

6. Have I packed a spare box or beeswax cloth?

69

HOLIDAYS

If you've made a lot of waste savings over the year, you might think that holidays are the one time you can worry a little less. But if you want to keep things eco-friendly there are lots of ways you can do this while on holiday. There are many beautiful campsites and hotels that are "green", running on renewable energy and striving to be waste-free. You can also try eco-tourism, where you spend time in a stunning location helping locals with green initiatives, such as beach cleans or building facilities. Around 8.8 per cent of carbon gas emissions come from the tourism industry, with airplane travel being a big sinner in that category. Why not enjoy a "staycation" – a holiday in your own country – and avoid increasing your carbon footprint?

SPECIAL OCCASIONS

INTRODUCTION

Some of the things that make celebrations so enjoyable – presents, beautiful decorations, charming wrapping paper and cards – are the same things that are a burden on our planet, and that's without all the unwanted presents and overabundance of food that will never be eaten. This doesn't mean that you have to struggle with austere birthdays and festivities though (and no, it doesn't mean that you get out of buying presents with the "I'm eco-friendly now" excuse). Instead, read on to find plenty of tips for beautiful, heart-warming and waste-free celebrations.

70

GIVE AN EXPERIENCE

Replace material presents with gifts of experiences. Gifting an experience means eliminating all of your wrapping waste and the risk that the present will head to landfill if it isn't well liked by the recipient. Gift experiences are also perfect for those people who have everything – you will be providing them with fun or learning (or a fun learning experience!) instead of unnecessary stuff that you know in your heart they don't really want. Plus, if you're buying an experience for two, you may be invited to share in the fun as well!

71

ETHICAL CONSUMERISM

If you have a friend or relative that you think would prefer to receive something to open, there are other ways to purchase material objects that still help to reduce waste. Some people would love a gift from a second-hand store or retro shop if it were special in some way – perhaps something quirky and unusual, perhaps a specialist item from their childhood, or perhaps they just prefer the look or feel of used and old items. For loved ones that are decidedly not of this opinion, why not buy beautiful eco-friendly items? Lunch boxes, crockery and washing items made of bamboo are lovely to look at, and clothing made of hemp or bamboo is very soft to the touch.

72

CUT THE PLASTIC FROM YOUR GIFT WRAPPING

Once all the presents have been opened, that bright and beautiful gift wrap could be headed straight for the landfill. Sticky tape is plastic-based and not recyclable, and wrapping paper that is laminated (shiny), foiled (metallic), or covered in glitter is also not recyclable. If you're unsure about whether your wrapping paper can be recycled, try the "scrunch" test – if the paper holds its shape after you crumple it up then it is recyclable. Replace sticky tape with plain string, dyed string, yarn or natural raffia for an attractive and even retro effect. You can create your own recyclable wrapping paper using newspaper, old magazines, brown paper grocery bags or old maps. Cutting the paper with paper edgers (specially serrated scissors) creates attractive edges.

73

CLOTH WRAPPING

Furoshiki is a Japanese method of folding and knotting cloth around presents to create beautiful gift wrapping. It is tape- and pin-free, and the cloth can be reused for other packages or recycled around the house. There are folding and knotting styles for lots of different shapes, so you'll be able to use *furoshiki* to wrap most gifts. You can buy cloth designed to be used for *furoshiki* online, or any thin, attractive cloth will suit your purpose – second-hand stores are a great resource for suitable cloth in the form of scarves. Search online for guides to *furoshiki* methods and you'll find plenty of clear instructions including pictures – it couldn't be easier. *Furoshiki* is beautiful enough on its own, but you could make your designs really special by adding a sprig of flowers or greenery.

74

PRESSED OR DRIED FLOWERS

Flowers will compost in your home composter, but there are ways to squeeze a little more life out of them first, while also doing away with plastic non-recyclable ribbons and gifting decorations. Dry or press faded blooms from your house and garden (old bouquets would work as well). You can press flowers between the pages of old books or dry them on a low heat on an oven tray. Once they are ready store them in an airtight container. These will make beautiful additions to gifts wrapped in paper or cloth.

75

THROWING AN ECO PARTY

You might want to throw a party with lots of guests but you simply don't have the crockery to cater for everyone. Always buy paper plates and cups instead of plastic plates and cups. Some eco brands offer paper plates and cups that will biodegrade in home composting, while standard paper cups and plates should biodegrade in landfill over the course of around three months. Dirty paper crockery can't be recycled as the food and grease marks would contaminate the paper stock. If you have the storage space, purchase a bulk amount of crockery from second-hand stores. You can keep them packed away most of the time and get them out for large parties. For a bit of fun, mismatch them and include quirky ones too!

76) ORANGE SLICE CHRISTMAS DECORATIONS

You won't want to use wasteful and plastic-heavy shop-bought Christmas decorations once you master the art of DIY Christmas decorations. These orange slice baubles are very cheap and easy to make and will fill your home with a lovely festive scent. No waste is involved in their creation and they can be disposed of in the compost.

You will need: Three large oranges.

Preheat the oven to 150°C/300°F.

Line several shallow baking sheets with parchment paper.

Slice the oranges thinly (no thicker than half a centimetre) and lay flat on the baking sheets. Bake for 2–4 hours, turning regularly.

When the slices are dry to the touch, remove and cool. Press a hole through the slice and thread ribbon through to hang.

77) SALT DOUGH DECORATIONS

Creating salt dough decorations is the perfect Christmas craft, especially with children. You can also make these as sophisticated as you like, utilizing stamps, acrylic paints and other decorative elements.

You will need: 1 cup flour, 1 cup salt, 1 cup room temperature water, cookie cutters, acrylic paint, stamps, ink, glitter.

Preheat the oven to 150°C/300°F.

Mix together the dry ingredients and slowly add the water, stirring to combine.

Once the dough is formed, remove from bowl and knead on a lightly floured surface until smooth.

Mould the dough into shapes or use a rolling pin to roll it to half a centimetre's thickness and use a cookie cutter to cut shapes.

Bake for at least 3 hours (larger, thicker shapes will need longer). If you're stamping designs on to the dough, do so before baking. Once baked and cooled, paint with acrylic paint and decorate with glitter.

78

USE YOUR CHRISTMAS LEFTOVERS

Stop! Don't scrape those Christmas dinner leftovers into the bin! If you suspect that you've cooked enough food at Christmas to feed a family for a week then you probably have. Incorporate any leftovers into your cooking for the next few days and save on food waste. Beat an egg and mix it in with chopped Christmas veg and a handful of herbs then fry it for a delicious – and thankfully light – next-day brunch. Leftover turkey and meat scraps can be used in the perennial favourite: turkey curry. You can boil the bones with water, herbs and veg to make a delicious stock. Even your fancy gravy can be frozen for up to three months (provided it isn't milk- or cream-based).

79

REGIFT THOUGHTFULLY

Don't discard unwanted Christmas gifts in your general waste bin. Second-hand stores and charity shops will accept almost anything as long as it is in good condition, although some stores are reluctant to take electronics. You could even host an "unwanted gift exchange" on one of January's many long, dull evenings (but take care not to invite the person who gifted you your unloved gift). You'll extend the festivities for another day and just remember: one person's trash is another person's treasure! You can be eco-conscious by including gift receipts in the presents that you give. Sometimes the thought counts more than the actual gift.

80

CUT OUT PUMPKINS

Pumpkin carving is fun, but so much of the pumpkin is discarded and goes to waste. Pumpkins pump out a lot of methane when they decompose, so although they're suitable for your home composter, they're not exactly eco-friendly. Return to old traditions and swap your shop-bought decorative pumpkins for turnips – you can even grow them yourself. Turnip carving predates pumpkin carving, and turnips are a hardy and more eco-friendly crop. If you just can't resist pumpkin carving, reserve the insides to add to pumpkin pie. The seeds can be saved too – roast them and add salt and pepper for an ideal long-lasting snack.

81

GREEN SWEETS

Buy your sweets for trick or treaters the old-fashioned way – from a sweet store. The sweets in these stores are displayed in glass jars and scooped out into paper bags (you can bring your own, of course); this is much lighter on packaging than plastic-encased packets of sweets found in supermarkets and other high-street stores. You can make an attractive Halloween display for your seasonal visitors by putting your sweets in a glass jar, with tongs for trick or treaters to help themselves. If you'd like to offer paper bags then be sure to weigh them down with a stone so they don't fly away in a breeze.

82

EASTER DECORATIONS

It's not as common to decorate for Easter as it is for Christmas or even Halloween, but stores are increasingly pushing Easter merchandise, encouraging us to buy decorations that we'll use once and discard. Opt instead to find your decorations in nature. Decorate your house with cuttings from the garden; flowers work well and even great sprigs of fresh leaves and small branches will look charming when gathered together in a vase. You'll be bringing the beautiful, thriving outside into your home and marking the seasonal change to warmer, lighter days.

83

DIY DECORATIONS

There are plenty of ways to make your own Easter decorations, even if you haven't got a garden. Try making little eggs, bunnies, birds and blossoms out of the salt dough recipe on p.101. The decorations work well for any season – you just have to paint them with brighter colours! You could also try making your own bunting. Rifle through your cloth bag to see if you have any old clothes or sheets that would look seasonal for some spring bunting. You could even buy some cheap clothes and materials from second-hand stores. There are plenty of guides and patterns online and the only equipment you'll need is scissors, and a needle and thread.

84

HOME-MADE EGGS

Let's be honest, most of us could stand to eat a little less chocolate at Easter time. Cut down on wastefully packaged shop-bought Easter eggs by decorating or making your own. Paint blown chicken eggs with bright colours and patterns and use those for Easter egg hunts in place of small foil-wrapped chocolate eggs. You can use the yolks you blow out of the eggs to make an Easter cake. Buy chocolate wrapped in paper and melt it down to make your own chocolates to gift to your loved ones. You could even buy moulds from second-hand stores or repurpose old egg packaging to make DIY eggs. Sprinkle your eggs with chopped nuts and dried fruits for a beautiful effect.

85

THE BEST SHOP-BOUGHT EGGS

If you don't have time to craft your own Easter gifts this year then apply your shopping rules to the purchasing of chocolate eggs. Avoid eggs that come packaged in plastic, including the little bundles of chocolates that are packaged in plastic netting. Opt for eggs that are wrapped in tissue, foil or paper and that don't have any extra non-recyclable decoration such as wire twists, glitter or foiling. Old-fashioned sweet shops sell chocolates and goodies that are stored in jars, and their paper bags are often festively bright and beautiful, so they can be a good solution to eco-Easter worries.

86

WASTE-FREE CARDS

Cards can be one of the sweetest elements of any holiday or celebration – beautiful designs filled with loving sentiments. Despite being made of recyclable and sometimes compostable materials, cards are often packaged in swathes of plastic (individually plastic-wrapped cards – why?). Buy your cards from artists selling their wares at markets – the designs will be more original and they likely won't have the same packaging. If you are buying from the high street, look for bulk packages of cards made of recycled materials. Card materials, including lovely coloured card and decorations, can be bought in art shops with minimal packaging. Use these to make your own cards – your thoughtfulness will be appreciated.

87

CHECK YOUR FESTIVAL'S GREEN CREDENTIALS

Festivals can be a pit of plastic, water and food waste – but they can also be a lot of fun. You don't have to give up live music to live waste-free, but it will benefit you (and the Earth) to look into a festival's green credentials before choosing to attend. Most festivals will have this information on their websites – check the initiatives they have in place for green energy, recycling leftover tents and detritus, and disposing of their general waste. Carpool with friends or, even better, arrive via public transport or the festival's specially arranged transportation. Take advantage of the festival's green initiatives while you are there, recycling everything you can and making sure you don't leave any large items such as tents or mattresses behind.

88

ECO WEDDINGS

Yes, even your white wedding can be green! Apply all the waste-free tips you've learned in this book to organizing your wedding for the best chance of a happy day that's happy for the Earth too. Ask a florist about seasonal flowers and see if you can buy these locally. Buy your wedding garment from sustainable clothing companies or second-hand stores. There are plenty of websites that aim to match pre-loved wedding dresses with new brides. Try to make a lot of your own decorations and consider borrowing others from recently married friends. Many couples struggle to store their wedding decorations and will be grateful to offload – it can count toward your "something borrowed". Work with your caterer to plan a menu that is in season and grown locally too.

HABITS, SKILLS AND MINDSETS

INTRODUCTION

So far this book has made nearly 90 suggestions for how you can cut waste and help the planet. You may be feeling overwhelmed and unsure where to start. Don't worry: this chapter introduces some helpful strategies and habits for those getting to grips with their new eco-friendly lifestyle. You'll also find some excellent recommendations for charities and not-for-profit organizations that have some tremendous waste-reduction initiatives of their own and can support you on your journey.

FORMING HABITS

The best way to form new habits is to start with small and sustainable actions. Fold simple waste-saving actions into your daily routine and don't get disheartened and give up if you forget a couple of times. Initially you may only remember to compost your scraps once or twice a week, but that could grow to three or four times a week, and then more. Soon you'll be composting as part of your regular cooking routine. Cutting out things is as much a habit-forming game as learning to incorporate things. At first you may be tempted by a new set of headphones, but in adopting your new waste-free mindset, you'll instinctively notice the overabundance of harmful packaging around the desired treat, and you will think twice.

90

JOIN ORGANIZATIONS AND CHARITIES

There are lots of charities tackling the waste crisis, with many different causes, including cleaning up the oceans, reducing landfill waste, helping redirect waste in the food supply chain – and many more! Donating money to these charities can really help them in their battle to reduce plastic. Funds are required to buy advertising, stock up on resources, organize events in local areas, create informational materials, and much more. This is a great option for people who might feel overwhelmed by the burden of reducing waste – why not support the experts?

91

30-DAY ZERO WASTE CHALLENGE

The 30-Day Zero Waste challenge is a test to see whether you can get by for thirty days without generating any waste for the landfill. You can recycle materials and compost food waste, but you can't add anything to your general waste bin. This doesn't just target plastic, but it's a great way to help you break bad habits and rethink how you consume goods. If you'd like to rise to the challenge then there are plenty of useful suggestions in this book that will help you out. Why not write a diary of your experience to record any particularly tricky elements of going waste-free, so that you can seek ways around them in the future?

92

LEARN ONLINE

Our throw-away lifestyles have encouraged us to buy anything we feel like owning even if we don't need it, and throw away anything we don't need. This may save us time but, as we know, it won't help to save the planet. It also means a lot of us have lost the skills to maintain the items in our home. A zero-waster should always be thinking "Can I make this? Can I mend this?" Look online to find a plethora of tutorials that will help you learn the skills to rejuvenate your home, including sewing, tailoring, upholstery, basic carpentry, basic plumbing and miscellaneous DIY.

93

SPIRIT – AND VINEGAR!

There isn't much that white wine vinegar can't handle. This household wonder-material is a shortcut to cutting waste. Keep one big bottle in your house instead of a plethora of general and specialist cleaning products, and everything will be clean and sparkling. The acidity of the vinegar dissolves most mucky build-ups, including, among other things, grime on metal fixings, burnt-on build-up on cooking utensils, dried dirt, chewing gum and dirty shoes.

94

MAKE DO AND MEND

You may have thought about darning small holes and re-attaching buttons to worn-out clothes, but have you thought about patching larger holes and tears? Patching will help your clothes last longer – and help you purchase and dispose of less. There are plenty of traditional patches available online and in high-street haberdashery shops, but there are also lots of cool fashion patches that are widely available. Or why not make your own by cutting up old clothes? If your clothes are too worn for even the second-hand stores, then cut them up and use them as cleaning rags or spare cloths. You don't have to stop there though – knitted jumpers and tops can be unravelled to provide yarn for new clothes or decorative strings to add to gifts.

95

THOUGHTFUL TECHNOLOGY

You might be surprised to learn that streaming music and videos uses a huge amount of energy – more than downloading – so avoid this where you can. Plenty of streaming services offer you the ability to download programmes to watch or tunes to listen to later, so opt for that. Unless you need specific technology for work or in your day-to-day life, buy your gadgets second-hand. Think carefully about your technological requirements and don't buy the latest gadget if you won't actually use it.

96

THOUGHTFUL HUMANS

It's pretty likely that some people will be less understanding about your waste-free lifestyle than others. Develop strategies for dealing with these confrontations so you're not left feeling upset by them. For example, if people in shops or restaurants say no to your attempts at using your own containers or rejecting certain elements of packaging then you'll feel less frustrated if you have a plan B in place (you could have a script that you use to gracefully end the conversation, or have another shop in mind). Don't get angry at people who may not be as up to date on waste-free thinking as you are. Evidence shows that society is slowly coming around to the necessity of cutting waste – they'll get there.

97

FIND OUT WHAT MAKES SOMEONE TICK

If you would like to promote going waste-free and you want to persuade others to join your quest, pick your battles carefully. Start with a friend rather than a chance encounter with a stranger, and be mindful of where to start your campaign. If someone is mad about haircare, you're probably not going to convince them to give up all twenty of their must-have products for a solid shampoo bar. But they might enjoy gardening, so have them try out a water butt system or composting their scraps. An amateur chef might enjoy the challenge of cooking with leftover ingredients and your thrifty friend may be particularly interested in the savings to be made when they mend and upcycle their possessions.

98

WHAT ABOUT BIG COMPANIES?

Vote green with your money by opting to use companies with progressive, eco-friendly initiatives and waste-reducing policies in place. You can find lots of information about a company's environmental and ethical standards on their website. There are also a number of websites that will report how "green" a company is, breaking down their practices and policies into colour-coded charts and checklists. It's best to not just take a company's word for how good they are but check multiple sources, including news stories, to make sure they're living up to their promises.

99

KEEP UP WITH ECO NEWS

We are living in the age of excess, but luckily for us that also includes information! Once you start looking you'll find lots of information about how to live waste-free. There are plenty of websites and blogs online that can keep you updated, or you can subscribe to ethical magazines to keep yourself abreast of the latest information. These sources will update you on the latest technology and gadgets to help you on your waste-free journey; they also advertise verified eco-friendly companies and give you tips and tricks to refine your approach to living waste-free. Most importantly, you can use these sources to get in touch with other like-minded people so you'll feel part of a community.

100

LEARN TO COOK

Being able to cook is essential to successfully living a waste-free lifestyle. You can cut so much waste by using raw ingredients instead of cooking ready meals. It's a skill that will help you innovate when cooking with seasonal fruit and veg – the range of ingredients available to you will inevitably shrink depending on the time of year, so your recipe repertoire needs to grow to keep you enthused by the options available during the year. You can also learn to be a little bit daring and try new cuisines that you wouldn't have thought of before and even a few unusual ingredients that wouldn't usually find their way to your table. Living waste-free is all about turning challenges into fun opportunities.

101

STAY STRONG AND CELEBRATE YOUR SUCCESSES

Modern-day society is structured around buying and consuming, so living waste-free and saying "no" to the norm can be taxing on your frame of mind. It isn't easy to be different to most people around you. When you're tired, tempted or feeling guilty because you haven't been "perfect" recently, just remember that you're doing well for even trying! You – just one person – are trying to change the world for the better! Well done! Seek out positive news stories about how people and communities who have embraced living green have helped turn around environments and launch initiatives that have helped thousands of animals and people. Keep going – it's worth it.

If you're interested in finding out more about our books, find us on Facebook at Summersdale Publishers and follow us on Twitter at @Summersdale.

www.summersdale.com